Beautiful
Paper
Cutting

LARK
New York

An Imprint of Sterling Publishing
1166 Avenue of the Americas
New York, NY 10036

Photography by Christopher Bain
Art Direction by Elizabeth Lindy
Illustrations by Orrin Lundgren
Layout by Michele Trombley

ISBN 978-1-4547-0885-8

Distributed in Canada by Sterling Publishing
c/o Canadian Manda Group, 664 Annette Street
Toronto, Ontario, Canada M6S 2C8
Distributed in the United Kingdom by GMC Distribution Services
Castle Place, 166 High Street, Lewes, East
Sussex, England BN7 1XU
Distributed in Australia by Capricorn Link (Australia) Pty. Ltd.
P.O. Box 704, Windsor, NSW 2756, Australia

For information about custom editions, special sales, and
premium and corporate purchases, please contact Sterling Special
Sales at 800-805-5489 or specialsales@sterlingpublishing.com.

Manufactured in China

2 4 6 8 10 9 7 5 3 1

larkcrafts.com

Beautiful
Paper
Cutting

30 Creative Projects for Cards, Gifts, Decor, and Jewelry

Lark Crafts

LARK
New York

 18
 20
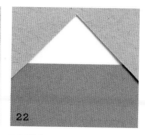 22
 24

 26
 30
 36
 38

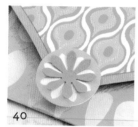 40
 42

 44

CONTENTS

 48
 50

 52
 56
 60
62

66

68

70

74

76

80

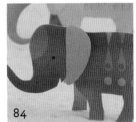
84

82

86

90

92

96

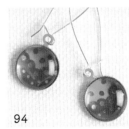
94

INTRODUCTION

Paper cutting has a long and storied history, spanning centuries and several different countries. Paper artistry is featured in a variety of places today, from art galleries and museums to children's books to hand-crafted cards and decorative items.

It's one of those techniques that can create a large spectrum of work, from high-end pieces to simple gifts. I happen to love the look, largely because it mimics block printing. But there are many reasons to love paper cutting . . . and to try it for yourself.

First, the basic steps are quite simple. Use a craft knife (or scissors or paper punches!) to cut paper. You can get started right away with the projects that use scissors and paper punches. For the paper-cutting projects that use a craft knife, you'll want to review the techniques (pages 13–15) and practice . . . a lot. Cutting with a craft knife takes a little getting used to, but you'll soon learn how to use the blade well, and we've provided helpful hints and tips along the way.

Secondly, you probably already have the supplies you need to get started: paper and a craft knife. And if not, you can get them quickly and for only a small investment. You'll find out how to turn a single sheet of paper into a beautiful and thoughtful gift.

Lastly, there's so much you can do with these techniques. Just take a look at the projects in this book. You'll find a mix of items for giving, from sweet gift wrap to cards; designs for colorful celebrations, like banners; items for the home, like framed pieces; wearable projects, like earrings; plus a few practical items to place and use around your home.

While the projects that involve a craft knife take a good bit of skill and practice, younger crafters can get involved with many projects, like the banner, the butterfly garland, and the hanging hearts.

If you're new to paper cutting, review the Paper-cutting Basics chapter that follows first, before you jump into the projects. The projects span a range of skill levels, so start with the more basic ones and work your way up. But most importantly, don't be intimidated by the final product. Sure, you'll need to practice and you'll need to be patient, but soon, you'll have your own collection of beautiful paper cuts.

PAPER-CUTTING BASICS

Getting started with paper cutting is relatively easy. You only need a few materials and tools, and the main techniques are quite simple, though they do require some practice. What you'll find on the following pages is a quick recap of the materials and tools you'll need as well as the basic techniques used for the projects.

Materials and Tools

The beauty of paper cutting is in its simplicity. There's perhaps no other craft that's easier (and as inexpensive) to get started with. The essential items—paper and a basic craft knife—are items you probably already have in your craft supplies. However, there are a few other items you'll need to make the projects in this book.

PAPER

For most of the traditional paper-cutting projects in this book, you'll want to use cardstock. It's easy to cut but sturdy enough to hold its shape, even when cut into thin forms. Most projects use solid-colored cardstock, though a few incorporate patterned paper. I tend to prefer the look of solid paper cuts, with their bold lines that resemble block prints. But why not bring some patterns into the mix? Or at least have fun shopping for them and building your supply? Some of the other papers included in this book include tissue paper and other store-bought paper items like gift boxes and gift bags.

CUTTING TOOLS

Craft Knife

A basic craft knife is essential when it comes to paper cutting, especially for cutting delicate interior shapes out. Any basic knife with interchangeable blades will do; however, there are many shapes and sizes available, including handles that are ergonomic or padded, and therefore more comfortable to work with. And do be sure to have many extra blades on hand. No sense in trying to cut intricate shapes with a dull blade: switch your blades out frequently for the best results.

Cutting Mat

You'll also want a self-healing cutting mat to cover your work surface. The cutting mat protects your work surface and also offers a little resistance while you're cutting through your paper. Again, there are many options on the market: consider the size of the pieces you work on as well as the size of your work surface when you're picking one out.

Scissors

Standard scissors, decorative-edge scissors, and a craft knife

You'll want a nice pair of sharp scissors to complete your paper-cutting projects. I like to use a smaller pair for really intricate work. A few pairs with specialty edges like scallops and zigzags might also come in handy.

Paper Punches

Assorted paper punches

The projects in this book use a variety of decorative paper punches and basic hole punches. From decorative corners to dotted or scalloped edgings to single motifs like flowers and butterflies, you'll want to have a few paper punches on hand. They're relatively affordable and easy to find, available in most major craft chains.

Rulers

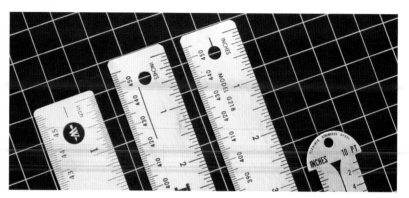

Assorted rulers

For cutting straight lines, a metal ruler is your best bet. It provides a perfect guideline when you're cutting straight lines. Don't think about using a plastic ruler instead: you'll carve it right up!

ADHESIVES

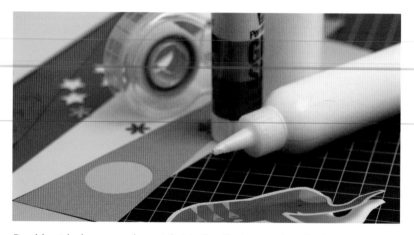

Double-sided tape, a glue stick, Modge Podge, and craft glue

The projects in this book use a variety of basic craft glue, glue sticks, tape (including double-sided tape), Mod Podge™, and adhesive strips. Tape is fine for many projects that will be framed or only used once, like a card. Glue and adhesive strips will provide a stronger bond, while Mod Podge is perfect when you're applying one layer to another and as a final top coat. If you're going the Mod Podge route, you'll also need a foam brush or a general craft brush on hand.

Basic Techniques

Clockwise: metal ruler, transfer paper, assorted cardstock, and craft knives

Here's a quick review of the main techniques used in the projects in this book. All of the projects are geared toward a beginning paper crafter, so you should be able to jump right in and get started even if you don't have a lot of experience with paper. That said, you'll still need to practice some of these techniques before mastering them.

WORKING WITH TEMPLATES

This is your first step in creating most of the projects in this book, as most of them involve templates. After you've enlarged and copied the templates from the back of the book, there are a few techniques to transfer those lines to the paper you'll cut out.

Two additional tips before you get started: Be sure to reverse the templates and patterns first, especially text. Also remember

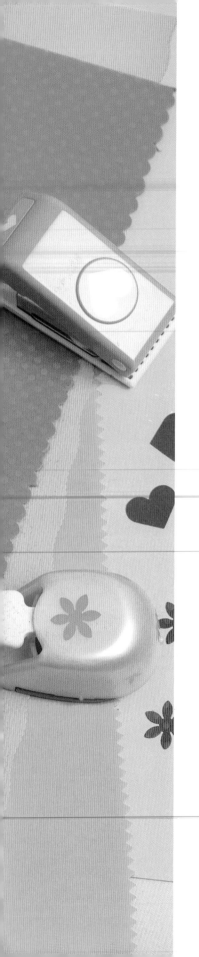

to work on the backside of the paper so your transfer lines won't show in the final design.

Cut out the shapes from the regular copy paper, place them on your cardstock, and trace around them.

Trace the design on the copy paper several times over with a pencil. Place it on the backside of the cardstock and rub the back of the traced design to transfer the lines.

Use carbon copy paper. Lay the design over the carbon copy paper and lay both over the backside of the cardstock (again, reversing if you need to). Trace over the lines of the designs to transfer them to the cardstock.

Once you've transferred the design, you're ready to cut it out.

PAPER CUTTING

This technique is as basic as it sounds: You use scissors and a craft knife to cut through paper. I like to use a combination of both actually: I use the craft knife on interior shapes and then scissors to cut my overall shape out. Here are a few tips to make that job easier, especially when you're dealing with intricate shapes and patterns.

First step: make sure you're working with a nice, sharp blade.

To make a basic cut, pull your craft knife along the paper instead of pushing it.

For straight lines, use a metal ruler as a guide. Simply line up the ruler along the line you'd like to cut and pull the blade of the craft knife along it.

For curves, try moving the paper and keeping your knife stationary.

To avoid tearing, press the paper down with your finger behind the blade, moving it along (again, behind the blade) as you cut.

Start with the most intricate part of the design. If you make a mistake, you can start over early in the process rather than when you're approaching your last (and hardest!) step.

And . . . that's pretty much it. It's a simple process but you'll need to start small, practice a lot, and work your way up to more complicated designs. You'll learn more about how the craft knife works and how different papers react to cutting as you go. But in all of this, have patience. And work slowly.

Paper-cutting Safety

Sharp blades, intricate shapes, intense focus, and your fingers: this could be a recipe for disaster if you're not super careful! Here are a few safety tips to keep in mind while you're working.

- Maintain your awareness of where your fingers are at all times.
- Hold the paper behind the blade.
- Always work on a cutting mat.
- Work slowly and with as few distractions as possible. (No kitty on the craft table!)
- Take breaks: this will help you stay focused.
- Store your craft knife in a secure place, preferably with the tip cover in place.
- Carefully dispose of old blades by placing them in a small box or taping them to stiff paper.

TEARING

There's no better way to get a nice textured edge than by tearing, as featured in the Ocean Sunset project (page 52). You'll want to make sure you're using paper with a colored core or paper that is colored on both sides for this technique. It can be somewhat difficult to control the direction of tears, so practice first with scrap paper before working with your fancy cardstock. Simply hold the paper in one hand and tear it with your dominant hand, leaving a rough edge.

FOLDING

A few projects in this book incorporate folding. For a nice hard fold, score your fold line first and then use a bone folder or the back of a spoon to complete and smooth the fold. If you need to create a channel in your fold, as in the Happy Birthday Banner project (page 44), fold your paper over a length of thick wire or thin rod.

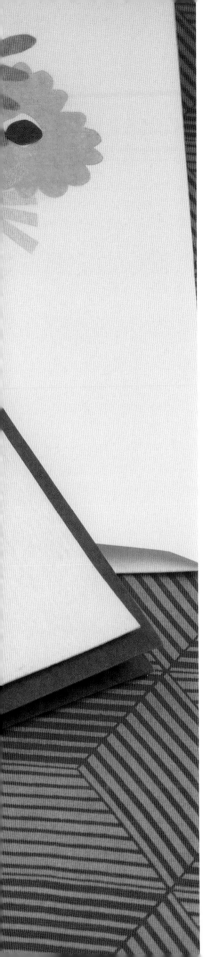

CARDS

CELEBRATION
GARLAND CARD

DESIGNER: ALI HARRISON

A pretty little garland and a sweet message make this the perfect card for a birthday or anniversary celebration. Use patterned paper behind the cut garland for added punch and interest.

Materials & Tools

- Templates (page 100)
- Pencil
- Brown flat card, size A2, 4¼ x 5½ inches (10.8 x 14 cm)
- Craft knife
- Cutting mat
- Double-sided tape
- Green fold-over card, size A2, 4¼ x 5½ inches (10.8 x 14 cm)

INSTRUCTIONS

1. Using the template, transfer or trace the garland and the words on the brown flat card: this will now be the backside of the card. Each triangular flag should be drawn separately from the string above. The bows should also be separate shapes. The larger the design, the easier it will be to cut.

Note: Remember that the words will have to be printed backward.

2. Since mistakes with lettering usually can't be fixed, cut out the letters first with a craft knife, working on top of the cutting mat.

3. Next, cut out the garland pattern above the lettering.

4. Place double-sided tape onto the four corners on the back of the brown card.

5. Adhere the brown card to the green fold-over card. Line up two of the corners first, and then press down to ensure straight placement.

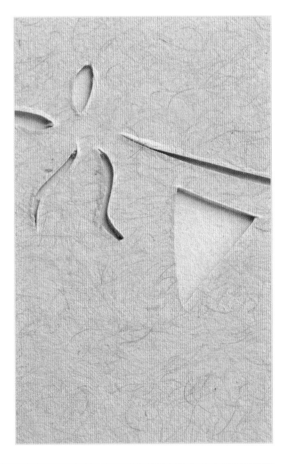

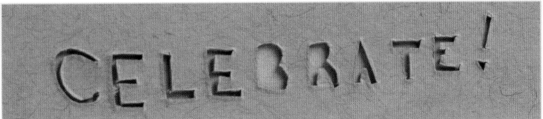

IT'S RAINING
LOVE CARD

DESIGNER: ALI HARRISON

A downpour of delicate hearts is a simple way to express a range of emotions, from love through hardship to a showering of affection. Even better: a bit of soft color peeks out from behind the cut shapes.

Materials & Tools

- Template (page 100)
- Pencil
- Brown flat card, size A2, 4¼ x 5½ inches (10.8 x 14 cm)
- Craft knife
- Cutting mat
- Blue fold-over card, size A2, 4¼ x 5½ inches (10.8 x 14 cm)
- Double-sided tape

INSTRUCTIONS

1. Using the template, transfer or trace the design onto the brown flat card: this will now be the backside of the card. The larger the design, the easier it will be to cut.

2. Cut out the design on top of the cutting mat using the craft knife.

3. Place double-sided tape onto the four corners on the back of the brown card.

4. Adhere the brown card to the blue fold-over card. Line up two of the corners first, and then press down to ensure straight placement.

SNOW-CAPPED
MOUNTAIN CARD

DESIGNER: ALI HARRISON

Layered paper creates this graphic, bold, snow-capped shape, excellent for a fan of the outdoors or for anyone who appreciates a mountain landscape.

Materials & Tools

- Templates (page 100)
- Pencil
- Brown flat card, size A2, 4¼ x 5½ inches (10.8 x 14 cm)
- Craft knife
- Cutting mat
- Metal ruler
- Sheet or scrap of green paper
- Tape
- White fold-over card, size A2, 4¼ x 5½ inches (10.8 x 14 cm)
- Double-sided tape

INSTRUCTIONS

1. Using the template, draw or trace a triangle onto the brown flat card; this will now be the backside of the card. Use the ruler and the measuring lines on the cutting mat to ensure the triangle is straight and centered.

2. Cut the triangle out using the craft knife and the cutting mat. Use a metal ruler for straighter lines.

3. Cut a rectangle from the green paper, making sure it is larger than the triangle but smaller than the card width. Use the triangle piece you cut from the card in the previous step to size the paper.

4. Tape the green paper to the backside of the brown card. The placement of the green paper will depend on how much green and white you would like exposed on the mountain.

5. Place double-sided tape onto the four corners on the back of the brown flat card.

6. Adhere the brown card to the white fold-over card. Line up two of the corners first, and then press down to ensure straight placement.

ALL-OCCASION GREETING CARD

DESIGNER: CYNTHIA SHAFFER

A trio of colorful flowers creates the perfect anytime card. The bold navy background really makes the flowers pop, but try different colors and combinations to personalize your card.

Materials & Tools

- Templates (page 101)
- Sheet each of cardstock in navy blue, light blue, purple, and peach
- Pencil
- Craft knife
- Cutting mat
- White envelope that measures 4³/₄ x 6³/₈ inches (12 x 16.2 cm)
- White glue
- Ruler

INSTRUCTIONS

1. From the navy blue sheet of cardstock, cut out a panel that measures 9¼ x 6 inches (23.5 x 15.2 cm) and fold it in half widthwise.

2. Trace template A onto the sheet of peach cardstock.

3. Place the peach cardstock onto the craft mat, and cut out the shape using a craft knife. Cut slowly and carefully to avoid cutting through the fine lines of the flowers and stems.

4. Trace templates B and C onto the purple, peach, and light blue cardstock.

Note: The little light blue circles can be punched out using a ¼-inch (.6 cm) hole punch.

5. Use a craft mat and craft knife to cut out the purple, peach, and light blue shapes.

6. Trace template D onto the edge of the navy blue card, ¼ inch (.6 cm) from the right edge. Cut out using the craft mat and craft knife.

7. Cut a strip of peach cardstock that measures ½ x 5¾ inches (1.3 x 14.6 cm).

8. Glue the peach strip to the inside of the card, covering the rippled cut strip.

9. Place the cut peach panel on the navy card and center. Use a pencil to lightly mark the center portion of the flowers and the lower portion where the light blue strip will be glued.

10. Lift the peach panel off the card. Apply glue to the purple ovals and the light blue strip, and glue them to the card.

Note: The purple ovals will extend out from behind the peach flowers. The light blue strip at the bottom should line up close enough to hide the right, left, and bottom edges.

11. Carefully apply glue to the backside of the peach cutout and then glue it onto the navy card.

12. Glue the light blue circles to the flowers and the three little peach petals to the card.

CUT TISSUE PAPER GREETING CARD

DESIGNER: CYNTHIA SHAFFER

Tissue paper flowers create a dynamic pop of color on this card, especially where the blooms overlap. With bold black stems in dark gray, the card will deliver your cheery greeting with style.

Materials & Tools

- Sheet of cardstock in dark gray
- Sheet of watercolor paper that measures 5 x 6¾ inches (12.7 x 17.1 cm)
- Templates (page 102)
- Scraps of tissue paper in fuchsia, orange, and yellow
- Scissors
- Mod Podge (matte finish)
- Old paintbrush
- Craft knife
- Cutting mat
- Pencil
- White envelope that measures 5¼ x 7¼ inches (13.3 x 18.4 cm)
- Sewing machine
- Dark gray thread

INSTRUCTIONS

1. From the dark gray cardstock, cut out a panel that measures 10¼ x 7 inches (26 x 17.8 cm), and fold in half widthwise.

2. From the scraps of tissue paper, cut squares that measure between two and four inches (5.1 and 10.2 cm).

3. Fold each tissue square in half two times.

4. Cut out flower petals from the folded paper, starting at the bottom fold and radiating out from the folded corner.

5. Unfold the tissue square and you should have a flower shape.

Note: Even better if some of your flower shapes are wonky for this project.

6. Apply a thin coat of Mod Podge to a small section of the watercolor paper, and place a tissue flower on top. Apply another coat of Mod Podge over the tissue flower.

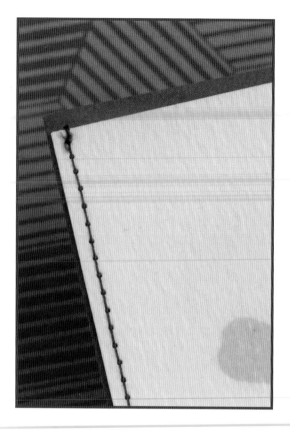

Mod Podge to the envelope where the flowers will go, place the flowers, and then apply another thin coat to the top.

7. Repeat with the other tissue flowers, overlapping the flowers to create a layered look. Set aside to dry.

8. With the leftover dark gray cardstock, trace the bee, stem, and center flowers' templates, and then cut the shapes out with a craft knife and cutting mat.

9. Apply a thin coat of Mod Podge to the card where the stems will be placed. Place the stems, and then apply another thin coat to the top of the stems. Repeat with the bee and the flower centers. Set aside to dry.

10. Cut a few small tissue paper flowers for the envelope flap, using the same steps as above. Apply a thin coat of

11. With the leftover dark gray cardstock, trace the envelope stem and center flowers' templates, and then cut the shapes out with a craft knife and self-healing mat.

12. Apply a thin coat of Mod Podge to the envelope for the stems and flower centers. Put the stems in place, and then apply another thin coat to the top.

13. Open up the dark gray card and align the watercolor paper along the center crease line, centering from top to bottom.

14. Machine-stitch the watercolor panel in place ⅛ inch (.3 cm) from the left edge.

WRAPPED INVITE

DESIGNER: CYNTHIA SHAFFER

*D*elicate colors and cutting wrap your message in a special way. Simply cut a large square, punch the corners, and place your printed invitation inside.

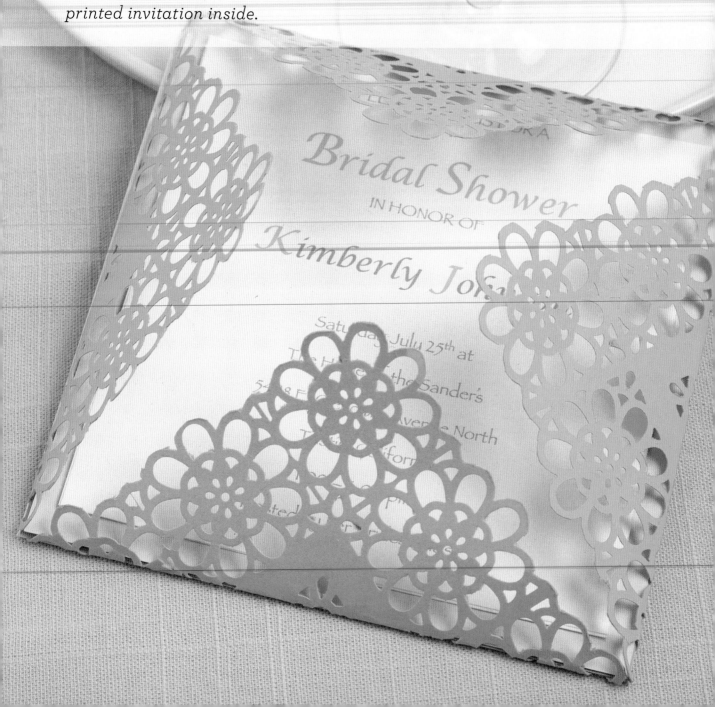

Materials & Tools

- Template (page 102)
- 2 sheets of coral cardstock
- Sheet of light green cardstock
- Floral paper punch
- Craft knife
- Cutting mat
- Small scissors
- Ruler
- White glue
- Printed invitation text on white cardstock

INSTRUCTIONS

1. Cut out four coral panels from the template.

2. Using the floral punch, make the first punch at the corner. Shift the panel to one side and punch out another flower. Continue until the entire edge has been punched.

Note: Use a decorative corner punch for a similar effect.

3. Make one punch in the middle of the panel.

4. Use small scissors and cut out the outer edge around the petal shapes, or use a craft knife and self-healing mat.

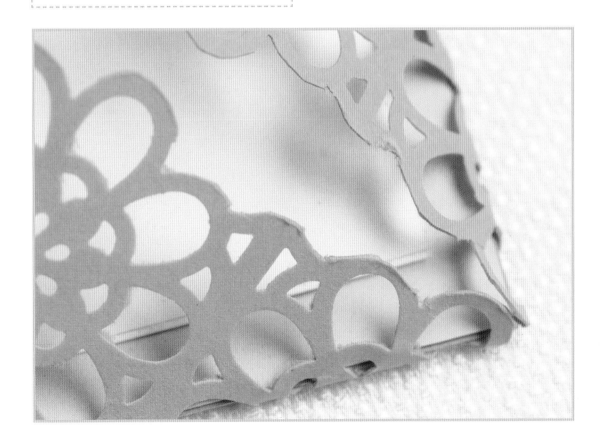

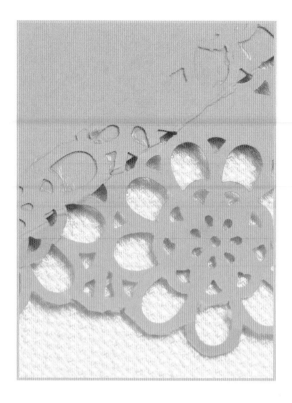

5. Repeat steps 2 through 4 for the remaining three panels.

6. Cut out one square from the coral cardstock and one square from the light green cardstock that measures 5¾ x 5¾ inches (14.6 x 14.6 cm) each.

7. Glue the punched panels to the edges of the backside of the light green square, overlapping them by ¼ inch (.6 cm). Set aside to dry.

8. Glue the coral square to the back of the green square, covering the overlapped punched panel edges.

9. Create text for the invitation that measures 3¼ x 4½ inches (8.3 x 11.4 cm). Cut out the printed text so that the panel measures 5⅛ x 5⅛ inches (13 x 13 cm).

10. Glue the text square to the green square, centering it.

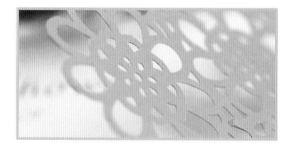

CELEBRATIONS

BIG BOW GIFT BAGS

DESIGNER: CYNTHIA SHAFFER

These gift bags are so pretty, they become part of the present. A punched border and a woven strip of cardstock create a custom decorative edge, but the steps are quite simple.

Materials & Tools

- Template (page 103)
- 3 turquoise paper bags, 3½ x 2 x 6¾ inches (8.9 x 5.1 x 17.1 cm)
- Scallop and dot edge punch*
- Scraps of cardstock in green, orange, and yellow
- 5 x 5-inch (12.7 x 12.7 cm) panel of white cardstock
- Craft knife
- Cutting mat
- White glue

*Note: If your edge punch does not have a hole punched out, use a ⅛-inch (.3 cm) hole punch and punch out holes along the edge, evenly spaced.

INSTRUCTIONS

1. Punch the top of the bag with the edge punch. Punch through the front and the back of the bag.

Note: Place your gift or gifts inside the bag before completing the next step.

2. Cut a strip of green cardstock that measures ¹⁄₁₆ x 4¼ inches (.2 x 10.8 cm), and weave it in and out of the punched holes. The strip will extend about ¼ inch (.6 cm) past the edges.

3. Fold the ends under and glue into place.

4. Cut a strip from white cardstock that measures ½ x 3½ inches (1.3 x 8.9 cm). Glue to the back of the top flap, allowing about ¼ inch (.6 cm) of the white to show past the edge of the scallop.

5. Using the bow template, cut out a bow shape from green cardstock.

6. Shape the bow ends around a cylindrical object like the handle of a paintbrush.

7. Glue the ends in place in the center. To hold the bow together while the glue dries, slip a paperclip over the center section.

8. Cut a strip of white cardstock that measures ¼ x 1¼ inches (.6 x 3.2 cm). Wrap this strip around the center of the bow and glue in place.

9. Fold the top flap over 1½ inches (3.8 cm).

10. Glue the bow to the top flap, centered.

11. Repeat steps 1 through 10 for the remaining two bags.

GIFT BOXES TO GO

DESIGNER: CYNTHIA SHAFFER

Make your gift that much more memorable with a custom cut gift box. Simply unfold the box, cut one side, back it with paper, and refold—and your gift is ready to go.

Materials & Tools

- Template (page 103)
- 3 take-out food boxes in green, orange, and white
- Craft knife
- Cutting mat
- Sheets of cardstock in turquoise, hot pink, green, and dark gray
- White glue
- Pliers
- Tag punch (optional)
- ⅛-inch (.3 cm) hole punch
- 30 inches (76.2 cm) white string

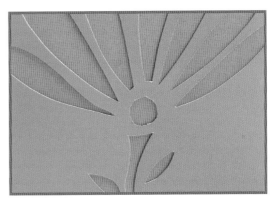

INSTRUCTIONS

1. Remove the wire handle from the green box. From the inside of the box, bend the wire back and slip the handle off the box. Fold the box panels flat.

2. Trace and cut out the flower template.

3. Place the template on the inside of the box, on a side that does not have the handle hole. Trace around the flower.

4. Cut out the flower using the craft knife and the self-healing mat.

5. Trace the inside panel, and cut the hot pink cardstock to size.

6. Apply a thin line of glue to the perimeter of the hot pink panel. Press the panel to the inside of the box, behind the cutout flower.

7. Fold the box back up and insert the metal handle. Using pliers, bend the handle back into place.

8. Cut or punch out a tag from hot pink cardstock. Punch out a small hole at the top of the tag with a hole punch, and then tie the tag to the box handle.

9. Repeat steps 1 through 8 for the orange box, except use turquoise cardstock for the inside panel.

10. Repeat steps 1 through 5 for the white box. Trace the inside panel on the green cardstock. Trace half of the inside panel template on the dark gray cardstock. Cut out the panels, overlap them, and glue them together and in place behind the cutout flower shape. Continue with steps 7 and 8.

GIFT CARD HOLDER

DESIGNER: CYNTHIA SHAFFER

*I*f *you're giving store-bought, make sure the wrapping is homemade. This custom holder helps you present your gift card in style.*

Materials & Tools

- Sheet of cardstock in gray
- Templates (page 104)
- 2 sheets of coordinating patterned paper
- White glue
- Craft knife
- Cutting mat
- Ruler
- Scraps of coordinating paper
- 1⅛-inch (2.8 cm) circle paper punch
- 1-inch (2.5 cm) flower paper punch

INSTRUCTIONS

1. From the gray sheet of cardstock, cut out one template A shape, transfer all the markings, and score at the fold lines on the inside of the holder. Fold the gift card at the scored lines.

2. From one coordinating patterned paper, cut out one template B shape.

3. Apply glue to the backside of the shape and adhere it to the front of the gift card holder, centering it.

4. From one coordinating patterned paper, cut out one template C shape.

5. Apply glue to the backside of the shape and adhere it to the gift card holder flap, centered and ¼ inch (.6 cm) from the point. This panel will overlap the back patterned paper.

6. While the glue is still wet, fold the gift card holder at the scored lines. The patterned paper may shift a bit. Set aside to dry.

7. Using a craft knife and ruler, cut along the inside marked diagonal lines.

8. Punch out one circle and one flower from your paper scraps. Layer the flowers and circles, and glue them together. Glue only the very center of the flower to allow the petals to be turned up.

Note: For variety, glue two flowers together and then adhere them to a circle. Or use the negative shape of a punch flower, and then punch a circle around it.

9. Glue the circle to the card.

Note: Make sure that only the top of the circle is glued ½ inch (1.2 cm) from the pointed end. This will allow the point to still poke into the front slit to close the gift card holder.

LOVE RIBBON WRAP

DESIGNER: CYNTHIA SHAFFER

This special message will make your gift stand out—and up!—from the crowd. Combining paper-cut letters and folding, simply wrap the ribbon around the package and tape it in place.

Materials & Tools

- Template (page 103)
- Sheet each of cardstock in navy blue and pink
- Craft knife
- Cutting mat
- Ruler
- Sheet of white copy paper
- Scrap of white cardstock
- ⅛-inch (.3 cm) circle paper punch
- White glue

INSTRUCTIONS

1. Cut a strip from the navy blue cardstock that measures 3 x 11½ inches (7.6 x 29.2 cm).

2. Trace the template onto copy paper and cut out around the top and side edges of the letters with a craft knife; do not cut along the bottom edge of the letters. Cut out the inside of the heart.

3. With a pencil, lightly mark a line ⅝ inch (1.6 cm) up from the bottom edge widthwise on the navy blue strip.

4. Align the cut copy paper letters along the line, and trace around the letters.

5. Cut out the letters, again leaving the bottom edge uncut.

6. Punch out circles along the letters as shown.

7. Punch out circles from the white cardstock scrap. Carefully glue the circles to the back of the letters, behind the punched out circles. Set aside to let the glue dry.

8. Trace the copy paper letters onto the pink cardstock, and cut out around the letters with a craft knife. Do not cut out the inside of the heart.

9. Glue the pink letters to the backside of the navy blue letters. Shift the pink letters up and to the left of the navy blue letters.

10. Wrap the LOVE ribbon around a box. Cut additional 3-inch-wide (7.6 cm) strips of navy cardstock, and glue the strips together so the ribbon wraps around a box completely.

HAPPY BIRTHDAY BANNER

DESIGNER: CYNTHIA SHAFFER

Display a happy message on this bright banner, complete with a paper-cut cupcake. Use different colors or a special greeting to personalize the project.

Materials & Tools

- Sheet each of pink and green patterned paper
- Templates (page 104)
- Pencil, scissors, and metal hanger
- 60 inches (152.4 cm) of green and white baker's twine
- 26 paperclips
- White glue
- Black broad tip marker (3 mm)
- Eraser and pliers

INSTRUCTIONS

1. Trace template A onto the backside of the patterned paper: seven times on the pink paper and six times on the green paper. Cut out the pennant shapes with scissors.

2. Roll the top of the pennants over a length of the metal hanger and crease with your fingernail.

3. Apply a thin strip of glue to the inside flap, leaving a small channel in the fold for the twine, and gently press it into place. Slip paperclips on the glued flap to hold it in place while the glue is drying.

4. Repeat steps 2 and 3 for the remaining pennants.

5. Measure 2 inches (5 cm) up from the point of the pennant, and draw a thin line in pencil. Draw another thin line ¾ inch (1.9 cm) from the first line.

6. In pencil, lightly draw the letters of Happy Birthday in this space.

7. Use a black broad-tip marker and draw back over the pencil letters. Erase any pencil marks that may be showing.

8. Straighten out a paperclip with the pliers, and then turn back one end to create a loop to create a rough needle.

9. Thread the baker's twine through the loop. Thread the straight paperclip through the top channel of the pennants to string them together.

10. Trace templates C and E onto the pink patterned paper and cut the shapes out.

11. Trace templates B, D, and F onto the green patterned paper and cut the shapes out.

12. Glue the template B shape to the backside of F. Glue C, D, and E above B, overlapping the layers as shown. Set the cupcake aside to dry.

13. Glue the back of the cupcake to the baker's twine on one end of the banner.

FOR
THE
HOME

FLOWER
FRAME

DESIGNER: CARLOS N. MOLINA

Despite its delicate shaping, this paper-cut frame makes a bold, graphic statement. Use the finished piece in a simple frame to surround a portrait or special drawing.

Note: Smooth, sturdy paper works best for this project.

INSTRUCTIONS

1. Transfer the pattern to the cardstock.

2. With a craft knife, carefully cut out the interior shapes.

3. To prevent tears, press the paper above the blade with the tip of your finger, and cut away from your finger.

Tip: Start with the delicate or difficult areas first, so if you make a mistake, you can start over early in the process.

4. Once complete, place your panel in a frame.

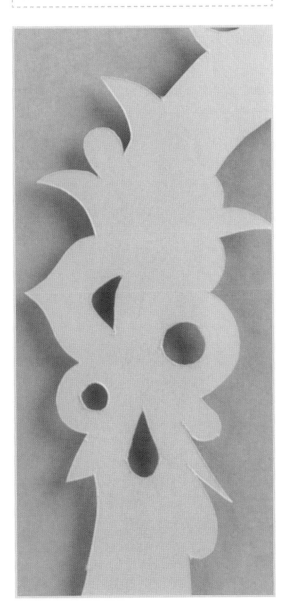

FLOWER PANEL

DESIGNER: CARLOS N. MOLINA

A bstract flowers dance above tall grass in this paper-cut panel. When you're done, place it in a simple frame with a solid background or paste it on a painted wooden panel or journal cover.

Materials & Tools

- Sheet of cardstock*
- Template (page 105)
- Craft knife
- Cutting mat

Note: Smooth, sturdy paper works best for this project.

INSTRUCTIONS

1. Transfer the pattern to the cardstock.

2. With a craft knife, carefully cut out the interior shapes.

3. To prevent tears, press the paper above the blade with the tip of your finger, and cut away from your finger.

Tip: Start with the delicate or difficult areas first, so if you make a mistake, you can start over early in the process.

4. Once complete, place your panel in a frame.

OCEAN SUNSET

DESIGNER: DEE DEE JACQ

This framed project combines the best of torn textures and tone-on-tone layers for an effect that is subtle yet striking, much like the ocean itself.

Materials & Tools

- Templates (pages 106–108)
- 8½ x 11-inch (21.6 x 27.9 cm) sheets of paper as follows:
  - 2 sheets of light blue
  - 1 sheet of dark navy
  - 1 sheet of aqua
  - 1 sheet of turquoise
  - 1 sheet of orange
  - 1 sheet of red
  - 1 sheet of pink
  - 1 sheet of magenta
  - 1 sheet of cream
  - 1 sheet of light brown
- Craft knife
- Scissors
- Small glass or circle cutter
- Double-sided tape
- White frame with 8 x 8-inch (20.3 x 20.3 cm) opening

INSTRUCTIONS

1. Using your paper cutter, cut one of your light blue sheets to 8 x 8 inches (20.3 x 20.3 cm). This will be your base and guide when making your piece.

Note: Frame sizes do vary slightly. You may have to cut your paper slightly smaller to fit your frame.

2. Cut your remaining 8½-inch-(21.6 cm) wide sheets to 8 inches (20.3 cm) wide.

3. Using the template and the dark navy paper, tear or cut your pieces to cloud pieces. With the smaller piece overlapping the larger piece, place both shapes on the blue background.

Tip: When tearing paper, wiggle your wrist slightly back and forth. This will create the textured edge.

4. Make the sun, trace a glass, and cut with scissors or use a circle cutter to cut two circles from the orange and red paper.

5. Tape the orange circle onto the red circle while allowing some of the red circle to show above and to the right of the orange.

6. Place the sun slightly to the left side behind the smaller dark cloud piece but in front of the larger cloud piece. Then tape it in place.

7. Using the templates, tear and cut the magenta, pink, and red paper clouds, and then overlap them to create layers. Place the magenta on the skyline first, followed by the pink clouds and then the red clouds. When you are happy with the position, you can tape these down.

8. Use the templates to cut your waves. Layer the waves as follows: turquoise on bottom, followed by aqua and light blue. They should overlap slightly to create added depth. Tape the waves in place when you get them into position.

9. Use the templates to cut cream foam and light brown sand. Tear, cut, and place the shapes at the base of the waves, starting with the cream and followed by the light brown. When you are happy with the placement, tape the layers in place.

10. Place the layers in the frame.

ALICE'S WARDROBE

DESIGNER: SILVINA DE VITA

A tiny wardrobe with tiny clothes and shoes creates a magical scene, protected from harm in a glass dome. For more design options, try printed papers for the clothing items.

Materials & Tools

- Templates (page 109)
- Sheet of plain paper
- Carbon copy paper
- Pencil
- Sheet of cream cardstock
- Craft knife
- Cutting mat
- Sheet of brown cardstock
- Paper glue
- Glass dome with base, approximately 13 inches (33 cm) tall

INSTRUCTIONS

1. Using the templates, copy or trace the elements of the design onto a plain piece of paper.

2. Place this sheet on top of the carbon paper and place the cream cardstock beneath it.

3. Draw over the elements with a pencil, pushing fairly hard. This will transfer the pictures onto the card beneath.

4. Cut out the shapes with a craft knife.

5. Using the same technique, lay the plain paper over carbon copy paper, and place both on top of the brown cardstock. Trace the wardrobe elements to transfer the shapes onto the cardstock beneath. Use a ruler so the rectangles are perfect.

6. To make the wardrobe, glue the top shelf, the hanger bar, and the bottom shelf in place between the two side pieces. Glue the wardrobe to the base of the dome.

7. Glue the clothes to the hangers and hang them on the bar. Hang the scarf over one side edge of the wardrobe.

8. On the shelf, glue the hats and the handbag in place.

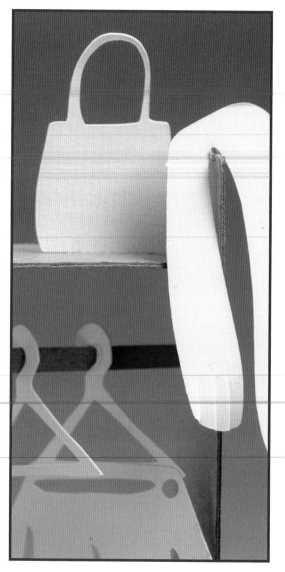

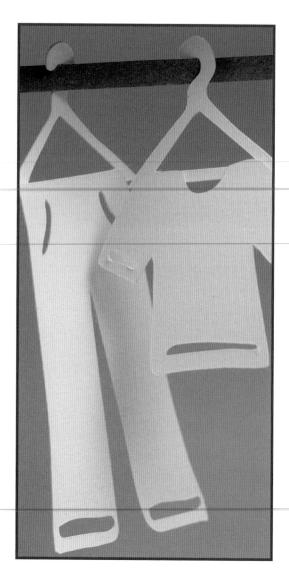

9. Glue the boxes and boots onto the base of the dome.

10. To make the boxes, fold the four tabs up 90 degrees, paste the edges together, and fill the box with paper scraps or anything you like. Paste the boxes to the base of the dome or on the shelf.

11. Put the glass dome over the elements.

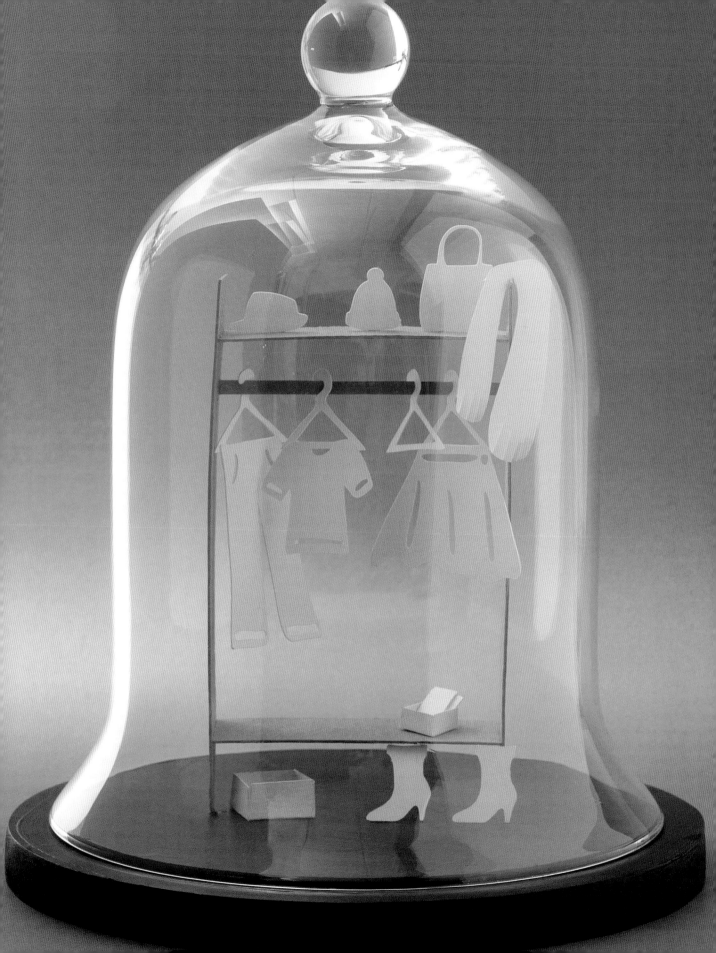

PARIS PAPER LANTERN

DESIGNER: REBECCA KEDBORN

The city skyline creates a unique graphic for this paper lantern. Cut the shapes or leave the cylinder whole, and then place a battery-powered tea light inside.

Materials & Tools

- Template (page 110)
- Sheet of paper that measures 8¼ x 11⅝ inches (21 x 29.5 cm) or one sheet of A4 paper*
- Craft knife (optional)
- Cutting mat (optional)
- Double-sided adhesive strips or glue stick
- Flameless candle (battery powered) or a votive in a glass container

*Note: Use two pieces of paper for the extra-large lantern.

INSTRUCTIONS

1. Make a copy of the template for the small lantern. Make two copies of the template for the extra-large lantern.

2. Cut out the shapes of the buildings if you prefer a more three-dimensional look. If you want the cylinder version, move directly to step 3.

3. Attach the double-sided adhesive strips (or a glue stick) on one side edge of the paper. For the extra-large lantern, apply adhesive strips to both side edges.

4. Peel the adhesive off, roll the lantern into a cylinder, and stick one side to the other.

5. Once assembled, the lantern is self standing. Slide the lantern over the light source.

Note: If you're using a votive candle in a glass container, make sure the glass is taller than the flame.

STICKY NOTE HOLDER

DESIGNER: REGINA SQUIER

This cheerful note holder will keep your desk in order and your supplies close at hand.

Materials & Tools

- Recycled cereal or cracker box
- Sheets of decorative cardstock
- Craft glue
- Brayer
- Round-edge paper punch or sharp scissors
- Heavy-duty hole punch
- 1¼-inch (3.2 cm) binding wire or metal binder rings
- Flower paper punch
- Craft knife
- Cutting mat
- Needle-nose pliers
- Stylus
- Molding pad
- Baker's twine
- Button
- ½-inch (1.3 cm) glue dots
- 3 x 3-inch (7.6 x 7.6 cm) sticky note pad
- Two 1½ x 2-inch (3.8 x 5.1 cm) sticky note pads

INSTRUCTIONS

1. From the recycled cereal box, cut two 3½ x 4¼-inch (8.9 x 10.8 cm) pieces and one 3½ x 3½-inch (8.9 x 8.9 cm) piece.

2. From the decorative cardstock, cut four 3½ x 4¼-inch (8.9 x 10.8 cm) pieces and two 3½ x 3½-inch (8.9 x 8.9 cm) pieces.

3. Using the craft glue, glue the cardstock pieces to both sides of each recycled paper piece. Using the brayer, roll the glued cardstock onto the recycled paper with a slight amount of pressure to secure it. Let the glue dry.

4. Using a punch or sharp scissors, round the bottom corners of all three assembled sheets.

5. Punch holes in top of all three layers, one at a time. Layer the assembled pieces, using the photo as a guide, and install the binding wire or binder rings.

6. Using your own punches, cut out flower layers. Using your rounded needle-nose pliers, grasp each petal, and, using your other hand, pinch the sides of the petal around the pliers.

7. Place the flower layers on the molding pad, and, using the stylus, twirl the center of flower, slightly adding pressure as you roll it; this will bring the petals up, adding more dimension to your flower.

8. Starting with the larger layer flowers and off-setting the petals, glue each layer on top of the other. Add a threaded button to the center of the flower using a glue dot.

9. Using glue, attach flower to front of holder.

10. Attach with glue the 3 x 3-inch (7.6 x 7.6 cm) sticky note pad to the bottom layer of the holder, and then attach the 1½ x 2-inch (3.8 x 5.1 cm) sticky note pads to the middle layer.

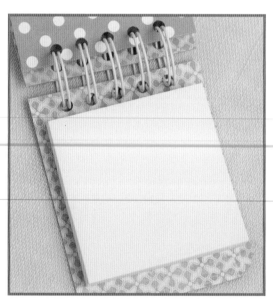

CITRUS SLICE COASTERS

DESIGNER: AMANDA CARESTIO

*T*hese sunny paper-cut coasters are the perfect spot for a cool glass of lemonade. Use them on a summer porch or inside to protect surfaces from condensation.

Materials & Tools
(to make one)

- Template (page 112)
- 5 x 3-inch (12.7 x 7.6 cm) scrap of orange, green, or yellow cardstock
- Craft knife
- Cutting mat
- Sharp scissors
- 5-inch (12.7 cm) square of patterned background paper
- Pinking shears
- 4¼-inch (10.8 cm) square white tile
- Mod Podge
- Foam brush
- 5-inch (12.7 cm) square of felt

INSTRUCTIONS

1. Transfer the template to the solid-colored cardstock and cut out the shape using the craft knife and cutting mat. Cut the interior shapes first with the craft knife, and then cut around the outside edge with the sharp scissors.

2. Using the pinking shears, cut the patterned background paper into a 4 x 4 inch (10.2 x 10.2 cm) square or to a size to fit the top of the tile.

3. Spread a thin layer of Mod Podge on the top of the tile.

4. Place the background paper on the tile and coat with another layer of Mod Podge. Place the paper-cut shape on the center of the background paper. Once dry, add several more layers of Mod Podge to seal it.

5. Once dry, coat the back of the tile with a generous layer of Mod Podge and place the tile onto the felt. Once dry, cut through the felt following the outline of the tile.

- July -

					4	5
		1	2	3	11	12
	7	8	9	10	18	19
6	14	15	16	17	25	26
13	21	22	23	24	♡	
20	28	29	30	31		
27						

WHALE WALL CALENDAR

DESIGNER: AMANDA CARESTIO

This paper-cut whale will keep you company all year long. Just copy the template and switch out the months as the seasons change.

Materials & Tools

- Two 8½ x 11-inch (21.6 x 27.9 cm) sheets of white cardstock
- Templates (page 114)
- Craft knife
- Cutting mat
- Pen or thin marker
- Pencil
- 8½ x 11-inch (21.6 x 27.9 cm) sheet of blue cardstock
- Craft glue
- Binder clip (for hanging)

INSTRUCTIONS

1. Transfer the whale template to the top half of one white cardstock sheet. Cut the whale out using a craft knife and cutting mat.

2. Print the month template onto the other sheet of white cardstock. Cut around the shape, leaving a thin border. Write in the month and the days on the lines provided.

3. Place the month grid on the white cardstock (with the whale on top). Draw short lines across the corners of the grid on the white cardstock beneath: these lines mark the slits you'll cut to keep the grid in place.

4. Cut along the lines you marked in step 3.

5. Place a thin strip of glue along the outside edge on the back of the white cardstock. Place this piece onto the sheet of blue cardstock, lining up the edges. Let dry.

6. Slide the month grid in place and place the binder clip at the top center of the panel.

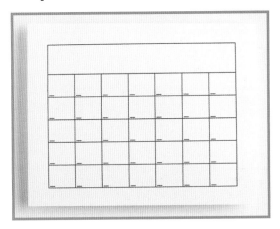

QUILLED LEAVES
VOTIVE COVER

DESIGNER: ALLI BARTKOWSKI

Fill your home with subtle light with this artful leaf-themed votive candle holder. The project combines paper cutting with some basic quilling for a dimensional effect.

Materials & Tools

- 12 x 12 inches (30.5 x 30.5 cm) black cardstock
- Craft knife
- Cutting mat
- Template (page 115)
- Copy paper
- Tracing paper
- ⅛-inch (3 mm) wide strips of black quilling paper
- Quilling tool (slotted or needle)
- Fine-tip tweezers
- Sticky note pad
- Craft glue
- Tape
- Votive glass and candle

INSTRUCTIONS

1. Cut a 4 x 12-inch (10.2 x 30.5 cm) piece of black cardstock. Score along the long edge every 3 inches (7.6 cm): when folded at the score marks, the shape will stand up by itself and form the votive cover.

2. Copy the leaf template and cut along the dotted line. Tape the pattern to back of the black cardstock, centered it on one panel between the folds and the top and bottom edges.

3. Using a craft knife, cut along the leaf pattern through both the copy paper and black cardstock. Carefully remove the taped pattern.

4. Cut a 3 x 3½-inch (7.6 x 8.9 cm) piece of tracing paper. Adhere it to the back of the cardstock with craft glue.

5. Using a quilling tool, roll six 8-inch (20.3 cm) strips of black quilling paper into coils and glue the end in place. Pinch the coil at both ends, between your thumb and finger in both hands, to create a leaf shape.

6. Place a puddle of glue on the sticky notepad. Using tweezers, pick up each quilled piece. Dip the quilled piece into the glue and tap the piece on the notepad to spread the glue on all of the coils. Place the quilled piece on the tracing paper in one of the leaf cutouts. Repeat for all six leaves.

7. Fold the cover around the votive glass and tape the ends together along the inside edge where they meet.

FOR THE KIDS' ROOMS

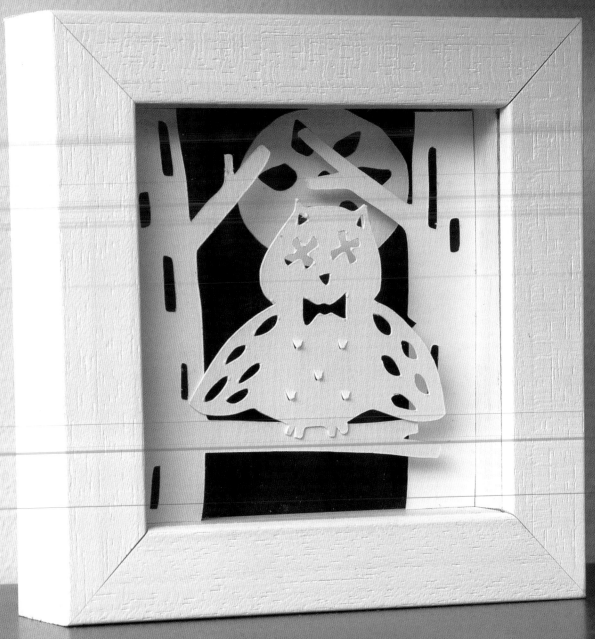

LITTLE OWL
SHADOWBOX

DESIGNER: SILVINA DE VITA

This project seems to tell a sweet and simple story that we can't resist.

Materials & Tools

- Templates (page 111)
- Shadowbox frame, 1¼ inches (3 cm) or more deep
- Sheet of plain paper
- Carbon copy paper
- Pencil
- Sheet of cream cardstock
- Craft knife
- Cutting mat
- Paint (any type) to create the background
- Paper glue

INSTRUCTIONS

1. Measure the height and width dimensions of your frame, and draw a square or rectangle of the same size on your paper. This will ensure that, once completed, your designs will fit into the box. It might be easier to draw a square for each element. For this design, the four elements will have to fit into a square of 4½ x 4½ inches (11.4 x 11.4 cm).

2. Using the templates, copy or trace the elements of the design onto the plain paper.

3. Place this sheet on top of the carbon paper and place the cardstock beneath it.

4. Draw over the elements with a pencil, pushing fairly hard. This will transfer the designs onto the cardstock beneath.

Keep in mind that once transferred, the elements will be flipped.

5. Cut out the shapes with a craft knife or scalpel.

6. The background can be anything as long it's the same size as the box. Paint a white piece of card (using purple paint, as in this sample project), or print and paste on a photograph or other image.

7. Fold both base tabs in half widthwise at a 90-degree angle. Glue along the bottom edge of the base and adhere this to the inside bottom of the box: you'll attach the trees to the folded-up portion in a later step.

8. Glue the moon to the background. Before you glue the trees to the box, place the owl on a branch.

9. Glue the trees to the base tabs. If needed, cut two more tabs for the tops of the trees and glue them to the box.

10. Close the box.

BUTTERFLY GARLAND

DESIGNER: CYNTHIA SHAFFER

A *paper punch makes quick work of this colorful butterfly garland. Simple folds take the punched shapes from flat to flying for a bright burst of floating color.*

Materials & Tools

- Butterfly paper punch, 2 x 1¾ inches (5 x 4.5 cm)
- Sheets of cardstock in a variety of colors
- Ruler
- 8 yards (7.3 m) of white string
- White glue

INSTRUCTIONS

1. Use the butterfly punch and punch out 22 butterflies from various colors of cardstock.

2. Cut a length of string that measures 1½ yards (1.4 m).

3. Make a mark on the string 5½ inches (14 cm) from one of the cut ends.

4. Continue marking the string every 4¼ inches (10.8 cm). You'll place a butterfly body at each one of these marks in a later step.

5. Carefully crease a butterfly on either side of the center body portion.

6. Lay the butterfly on a protected surface and apply a small line of glue down the center of the body. The butterfly should be propped up like a little tent.

7. Lay the string onto the line of glue with the mark centered in the body. Gently press the string into the glue line.

8. Repeat steps 5 through 7 for 10 more butterflies. Allow the glue to dry for a few minutes.

9. Carefully crease either side of the center body portion for the remaining 11 butterflies.

10. Apply a small line of glue down the body of the butterfly.

11. Press the butterfly onto the glued string and butterfly, matching up the center body portion.

12. Repeat steps 10 and 11 for the remaining 10 butterflies.

HANGING HEARTS

DESIGNER: CYNTHIA SHAFFER

*P*retty patterned paper gives these hanging hearts a folksy look that's easy to love. The design is quite simple, and this is a good project for involving kids and young crafters.

INSTRUCTIONS

1. From each of the double-sided papers, cut strips as follows. Cut two strips that measure 1¼ x 8 inches (3.2 x 20.3 cm), two strips that measure 1¼ x 10 inches (3.2 x 25.4 cm), and two strips that measure 1¼ x 12 inches (3.2 x 30.48 cm), for six strips total. Trim the edges with the decorative edge paper punch.

2. Cut an additional strip that measures 1 x 8 inches (2.5 x 20.3 cm). Mark this strip at the 4-inch (10.2 cm) point.

3. Stack the strips as follows, mixing the patterns as you go. Place the two 12-inch (30.5 cm) strips' right sides together. On either side of those, add the 10-inch (25.4 cm) strips. On either side of those, add the 8-inch (20.3 cm) strips. Line them up so that the short ends meet.

4. Insert the 1-inch (2.5 cm) strip into this stack, between the longest strips. Have the ends of the strips meet the 4-inch (10.2 cm) mark.

5. Staple the strips together at the 4-inch (10.2 cm) mark.

6. Pull all the strips down so that the other ends meet, making sure that the short end of the center 1-inch (2.5 cm) strip is flush with the other strips. Staple in place.

7. Punch a hole in the top of the 1-inch strip (2.5 cm).

8. Make multiple hearts and string them together.

HAPPY FOXES

DESIGNER: ELLEN DEAKIN

These 3D foxes are full of character! The positioning options are endless, and each one tells a different story.

Materials & Tools

- Templates (pages 116–121)
- Scissors
- Glue stick

INSTRUCTIONS

1. Copy the templates, carefully cut out the foxes, and glue sides A and B together for each fox. Note that each fox requires four to six templates.

2. **For Foxes 1 and 2,** fold the tab on the top of side B as indicated in templates.

3. Apply glue to the tab and, carefully lining up both sides of the fox, stick the tab to side A.

4. Glue the fox's nose and tip of its tail together.

5. **To make Fox 3 (the sitting fox):** Apply glue to the back of the fox and stick the shape back-to-back, leaving the front legs and chest unstuck.

6. Apply glue to the base of the tail and stick it in place.

7. Apply glue to both sides of the fox's head and stick the shapes together.

8. Carefully fold the fox's front legs out so it stands up.

ELEPHANT MAMA
AND BABIES

DESIGNER: ELLEN DEAKIN

This happy little three-dimensional family would be right at home in a new handmade nursery. Just cut the shapes with scissors and glue the shapes together back to back.

Materials & Tools

- Templates (pages 122–125)
- Scissors
- Glue stick

INSTRUCTIONS

1. Copy the templates, carefully cut out each elephant, and glue sides A and B together for each elephant. Note that elephant babies require six templates and the elephant mama requires twelve templates.

2. Apply glue to the top half of the back of each elephant shape (not on the legs) and stick each of the shapes together back-to-back.

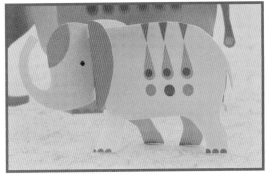

3. Cut out the ears and fold back the tabs. Apply glue to the tabs and attach the ears in place on each side of the elephant's head.

4. Splay the legs of each elephant a little so that they stand nicely.

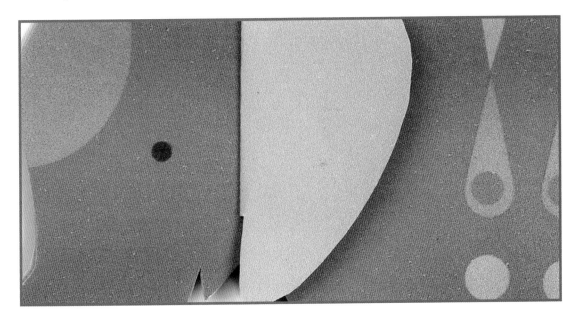

PAPER VILLAGE
MOBILE

DESIGNER: AMANDA CARESTIO

Create a sweet little village with paper cuts! Patterned paper peeks through the windows and doors for a playful project that's perfect for paper stash busting.

Materials & Tools

- Templates (page 113)
- 2 sheets of white cardstock (8½ x 11 inches [21.6 x 27.9 cm])
- Craft knife
- Cutting mat
- Metal ruler
- Sharp scissors
- Craft glue
- Scraps of patterned background paper
- Small paper punch
- Baker's twine
- Dowel rod or flat bar, about 24 inches (61 cm) long

INSTRUCTIONS

1. Transfer the templates to the white cardstock and cut them out using the craft knife and cutting mat. Use the metal ruler as a guide for all the straight lines, especially for the windows.

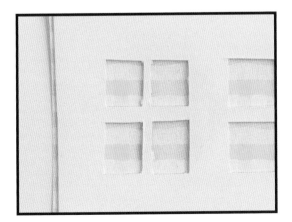

Tip: Cut all the interior first, then cut around the outside shapes with the sharp scissors.

2. Apply craft glue to the back of each shape and place them, wrong side down, on the scraps of pattern paper.

3. Once the shapes are dry, cut around each one, leaving a small edge of pattern paper border.

4. Punch a hole in each side of the square and circle shapes and in the top of each building.

5. Cut four 15-inch (38.1 cm) strands of baker's twine. String one shape and one building onto each strand. String the apartment building shape onto a strand.

6. Tie the strands evenly spaced along the length of the dowel rod or flat bar.

WEARABLES

PAPER DIAMOND BROOCH

DESIGNER: AMANDA CARESTIO

A small scrap of cardstock is all you need to create this sweet gem-inspired brooch. Switch up the paper and the background colors for a custom look.

Materials & Tools

- Template (page 112)
- Two 2 x 2-inch (5.1 x 5.1 cm) scrap of white cardstock
- Craft knife
- Cutting mat
- 1½-inch (3.8 cm) wood disk
- Metallic paint
- Foam brush
- Mod Podge
- 1-inch (2.5 cm) pin back
- Hot glue gun and glue or epoxy

INSTRUCTIONS

1. Transfer the template to the cardstock and cut out the diamond shape using the craft knife and cutting mat.

2. Paint the wooden disk with a few coats of metallic paint with a foam brush, letting the paint dry between layers.

3. Once dry, cover the wooden disk with a layer of Mod Podge and place the diamond shape on the center top of the disk.

4. Once dry, cover the wooden disk and the paper cut with additional layers of Mod Podge.

5. Glue the pin back in place on the back of the brooch.

PRETTY PAPER-CUT EARRINGS

DESIGNER: STEPHANIE PAXMAN

Create a pair of pretty paper-cut earrings using an electronic cutter or a simple paper punch. Coated with several layers of gloss, you can make a pair in every color.

Materials & Tools

- Scraps of colored cardstock
- Electronic paper cutter or paper punch
- Spray glitter
- Needle or thumb tack
- Gloss medium and toothpick
- Earring hooks

INSTRUCTIONS

1. Cut two paper shapes using the electronic cutter or the paper punch. Note that you can also hand cut two simple shapes with a craft knife.

2. Punch a hole in the top of each earring shape with a needle.

3. Spray the shapes with glitter and let them dry.

4. Cover the shapes with gloss medium using a toothpick. Drag any air bubbles to the edge with the toothpick.

5. Let both shapes dry for three to four hours, and punch the hole at the top one more time.

6. Slide earring hooks through the holes.

BLOWING BUBBLES
EARRINGS

DESIGNER: CANDIE COOPER

The colorful earrings make the most of the lacey edge of a paper-punched shape, combined with a bit of silver paper for full-on bubbly effect.

Materials & Tools

- Small paintbrushes
- 1 pair of bezel settings with acrylic cab, 3/4 inch (1.9 cm) diameter
- Green and aqua enamel paint
- Blue paper
- Lace edge hole punch
- Silver foil paper
- Scissors
- Decoupage medium in matte
- Multi-purpose adhesive with precision applicator
- 1 pair of silver kidney earring wires, 1¼ inches (3.2 cm)

INSTRUCTIONS

1. Paint the bezel settings with the green and aqua enamel paints inside and out, using both colors simultaneously to give the surface some variation. Don't forget to paint the backside.

2. Punch the blue paper with the lace edge hole punch, saving the tiny dots from the intricate lace pattern.

3. Lay the acrylic bubble piece on top of the lace edge paper so you can see approximately half of the lace cutout through the bubble. Trim away the excess with scissors.

4. Lay this small blue lace piece on top of the silver paper and trim around it so you can see the silver paper through the dots in the lace pattern.

5. Use the decoupage medium to attach the blue lace piece to the top of the silver paper piece.

6. Paint a little decoupage medium to the back of the silver paper piece and press it down into the bezel frame.

7. Apply a few more tiny dots of decoupage medium above the lace piece in the bezel frame and cover with the tiny blue paper dots.

8. Apply a bead of multi-purpose adhesive to the inside edge of the bezel frame and press the acrylic bubble piece into the frame. Adhesive may seep under the acrylic bubble here and there on the paper, but it just adds to the bubble effect.

9. Once the bezel pieces are dry, open the kidney earring wires and hang the dangles so they face forward.

STORY BEAD
NECKLACE

DESIGNER: CANDIE COOPER

Mix graphic papers and embossed gold sheets to create a stunning strand of 3-dimensional paper beads. Chain and accent beads complete this look that's great for everyday wear.

Materials & Tools

- Collage sheets filled with 1-inch (2.5 cm) imagery and script on thick paper
- Embossed paper in gold, 12-inch (30.5 cm) square
- ¾-inch (1.9 cm) circle hole punch
- Scissors
- Decoupage medium in matte
- Small paintbrushes
- Gold beading wire, 19 strand
- Brass spacer beads, 6 mm
- 4 gunmetal round beads, 12 mm
- 3 gunmetal round beads, 15 mm
- 2 gunmetal crimp beads
- Crimping pliers
- 4 solid coiled antique brass links, 10 mm
- 6 gunmetal jump rings, 6 mm
- Chain nose pliers
- 2 woven antique brass links, 18 mm
- Gunmetal chain, 1 yard (1 m) approximately
- Wire cutters

INSTRUCTIONS

1. Punch 48 discs each from the collage sheets and the gold paper with the ¾-inch (1.9 cm) hole punch for a total of 96 paper discs. It takes 12 paper-punched discs to make one bead.

2. Fold each disc in half and crease the fold with the edge of your scissors (or a bone folder if you have one) so it's nice and flat.

3. Pair six gold pieces with six image pieces.

4. To make one bead, paint a layer of decoupage medium on the outside half of one paper disc and glue the next disc to it so it sits perfectly in line with the first, alternating between the collage and gold paper discs. Repeat until you have all twelve pieces attached in this manner. Finish by painting decoupage medium to the last side of the disc and pressing it to the first disc, completing the round. The decoupage medium dries quickly, so no need to worry about clamping.

5. Repeat for the remaining seven beads.

6. String one brass spacer bead, paper bead, brass spacer bead, and 12 mm gunmetal bead onto the wire. Repeat this pattern

for all the beads, alternating between 12 and 15 mm gunmetal beads.

7. String a crimp bead onto both ends of the beading wire.

8. Thread one end of wire through a coiled ring and back through the crimp bead. Slide the crimp bead up next to the ring so there is still plenty of space for the ring to move freely.

9. Crimp the bead with crimping pliers by first placing it in the U-shaped notch on the crimping pliers and pressing the handles together on the pliers, and then turning it ninety degrees and placing it in the eye-shaped notch to fold the crimp over.

10. Slide all the beads next to the finished crimped end and repeat for the opposite side.

11. Open a jump ring using chain nose pliers from side to side and connect a woven link to the coiled link. Repeat attaching a second coiled link to the woven link.

12. Repeat for the opposite side of the necklace.

13. Fold the chain piece over and attach the two loose ends of chain to the coiled link with a jump ring.

14. Make adjustments to the chain length, removing some with industrial wire cutters if need be, and attach the opposite side of the necklace with a jump ring.

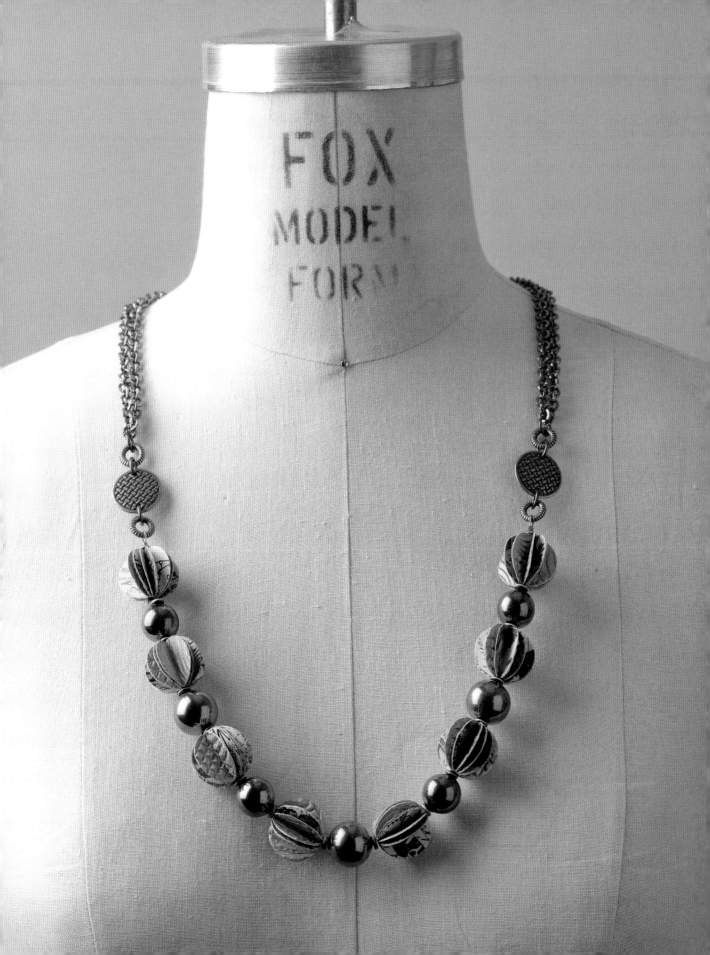

TEMPLATES

CELEBRATION GARLAND CARD
ACTUAL SIZE

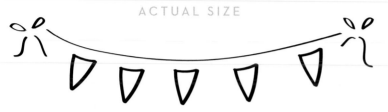

!ƎTAЯ8Ǝ⅃ƎↃ

SNOW-CAPPED MOUNTAIN CARD
ACTUAL SIZE

IT'S RAINING LOVE CARD
ACTUAL SIZE

ALL-OCCASION GREETING CARD–A
ACTUAL SIZE

ALL-OCCASION GREETING CARD–B
ACTUAL SIZE

ALL-OCCASION GREETING CARD–C
ACTUAL SIZE

ALL-OCCASION GREETING CARD–D
ACTUAL SIZE

CUT TISSUE PAPER GREETING CARD

WRAPPED INVITE
ENLARGE 150%

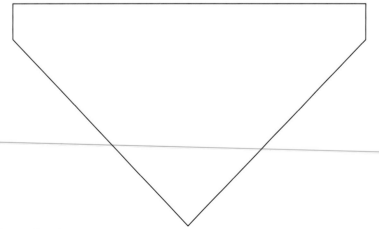

BIG BOW
GIFT BAG
ACTUAL SIZE

GIFT BOX
TO GO
ACTUAL SIZE

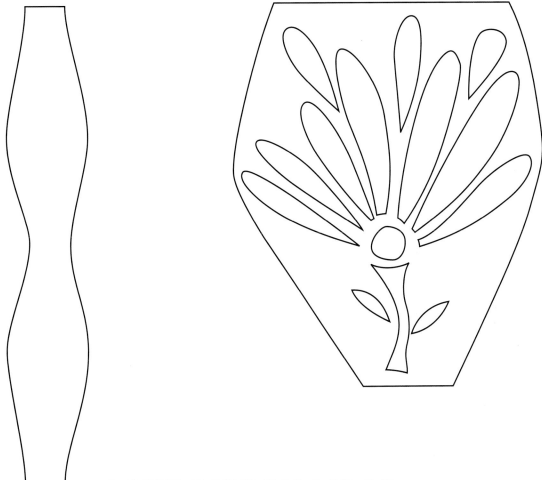

LOVE RIBBON WRAP
ACTUAL SIZE

GIFT CARD HOLDER

ENLARGE 200%

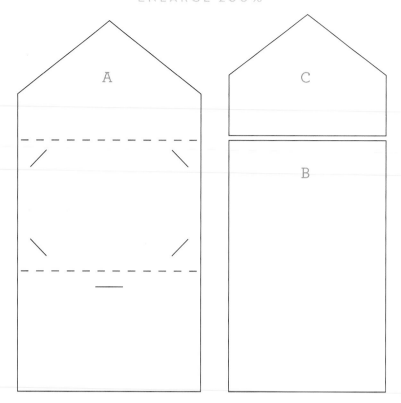

HAPPY BIRTHDAY BANNER

ENLARGE 200%

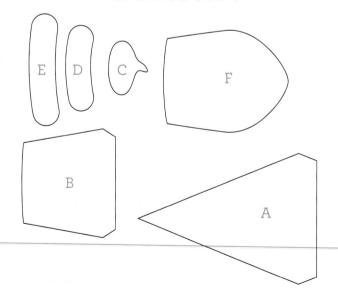

FLOWER FRAME
ENLARGE 200%

FLOWER PANEL
ENLARGE 200%

OCEAN SUNSET

ENLARGE 200%

NAVY
CLOUD

NAVY
CLOUD

ENLARGE 200%

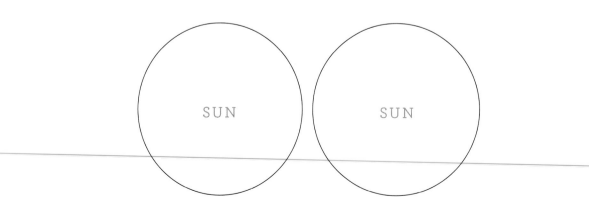

SUN

SUN

OCEAN SUNSET

ENLARGE 200%

RED CLOUD

ENLARGE 200%

MAGENTA CLOUD

ENLARGE 200%

PINK CLOUD

ENLARGE 200%

TURQUOISE WAVE

OCEAN SUNSET

ENLARGE 200%

LIGHT BLUE WAVE

ENLARGE 200%

AQUA WAVE

ENLARGE 200%

CREAM FOAM

ENLARGE 200%

LIGHT BROWN SAND

ALICE'S WARDROBE

ENLARGE 200%

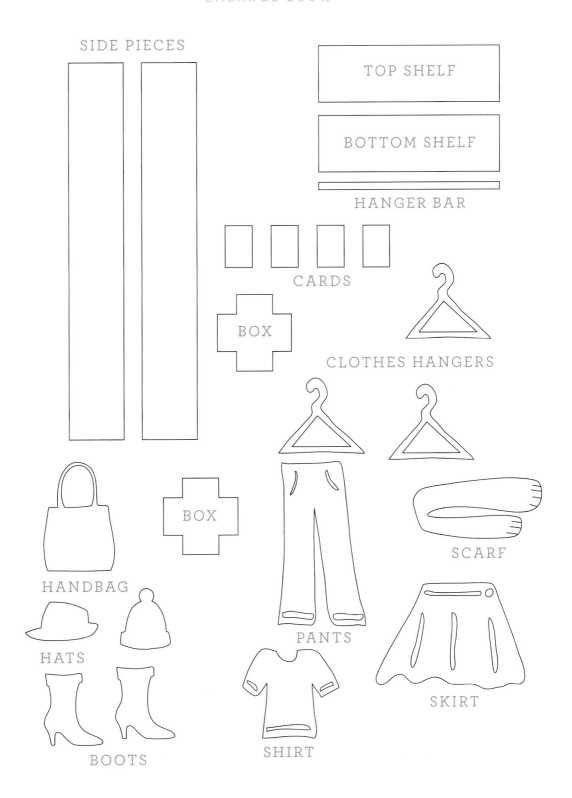

SIDE PIECES

TOP SHELF

BOTTOM SHELF

HANGER BAR

CARDS

BOX

CLOTHES HANGERS

HANDBAG

BOX

PANTS

SCARF

SKIRT

HATS

BOOTS

SHIRT

LITTLE OWL SHADOWBOX

ENLARGE 200%

MOON

OWL

TABS

TREES

CITRUS SLICE COASTERS

ACTUAL SIZE

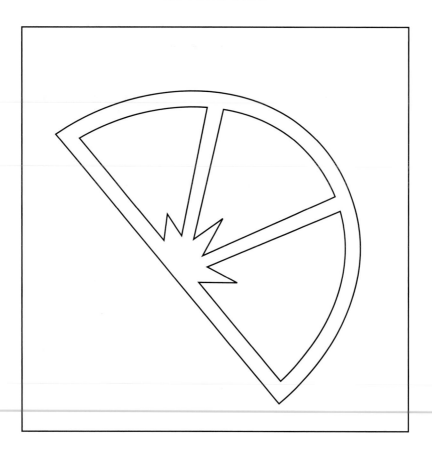

PAPER DIAMOND BROOCH

ACTUAL SIZE

WHALE WALL CALENDAR-A
ACTUAL SIZE

WHALE WALL CALENDAR-B
ACTUAL SIZE

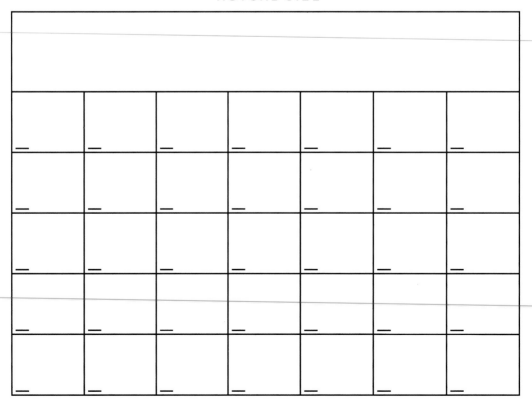

QUILLED LEAVES VOTIVE COVER
ACTUAL SIZE

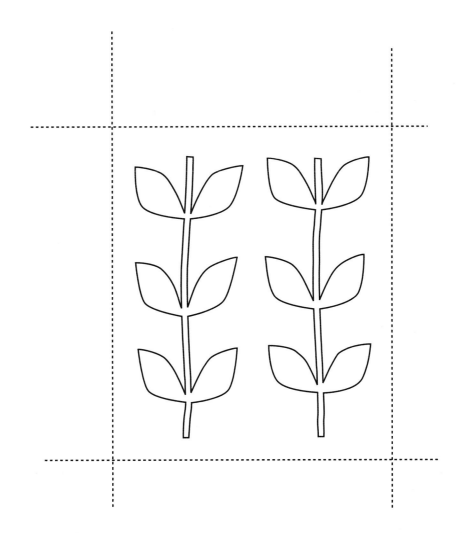

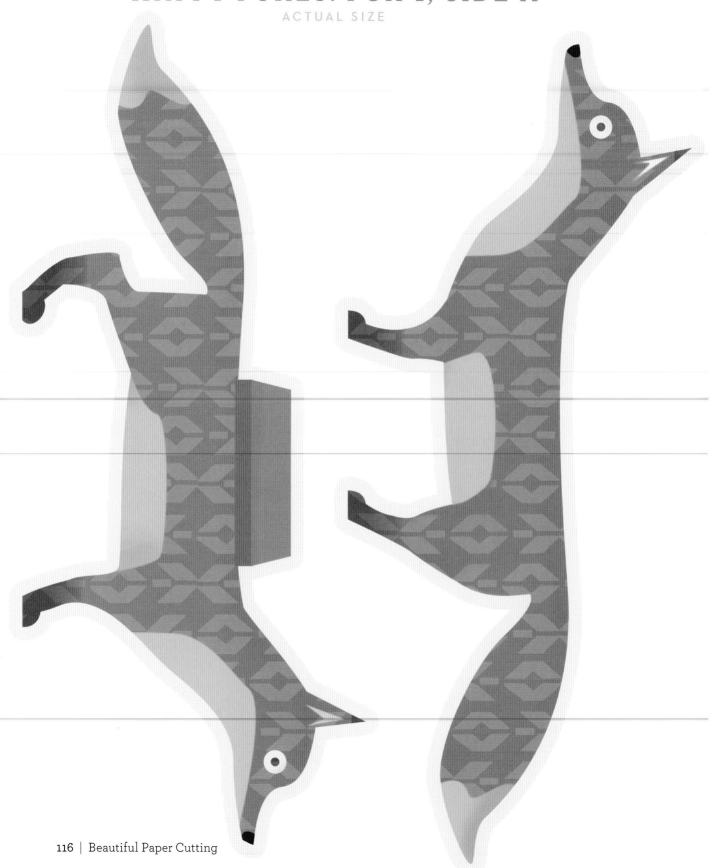

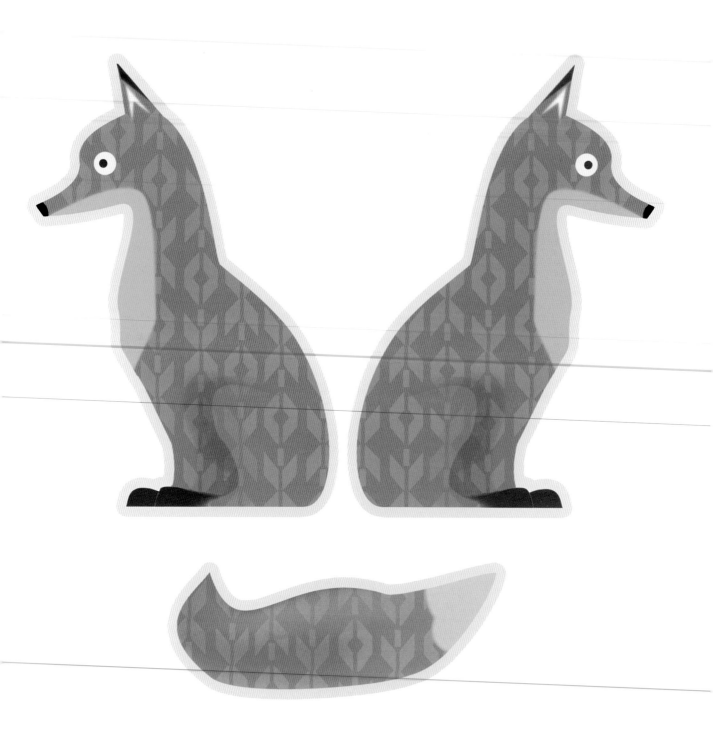

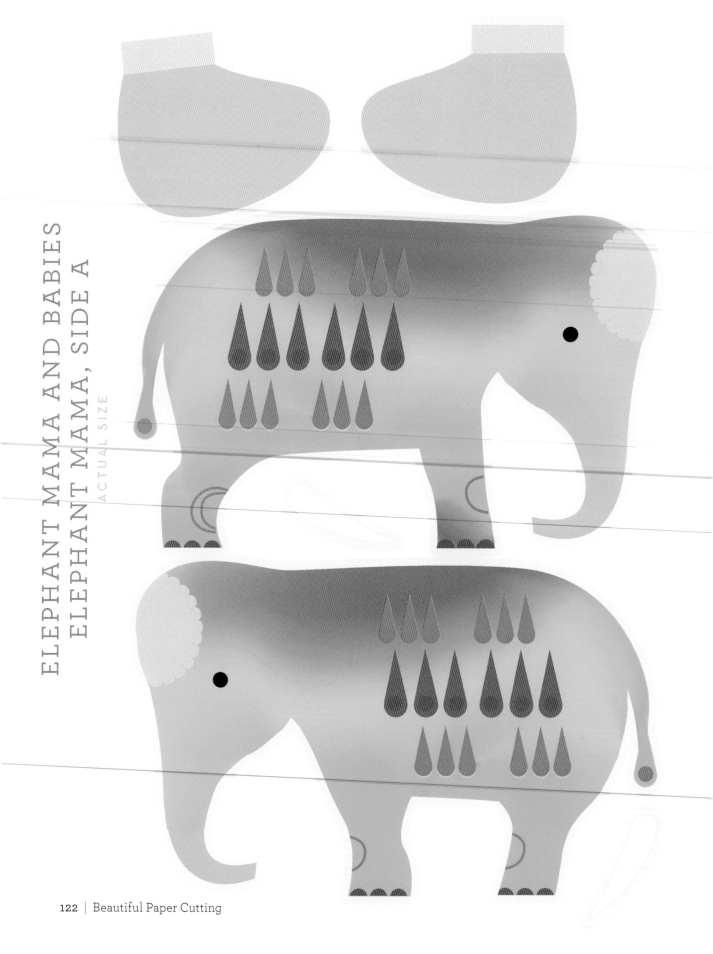

ELEPHANT MAMA AND BABIES
ELEPHANT MAMA, SIDE A
ACTUAL SIZE

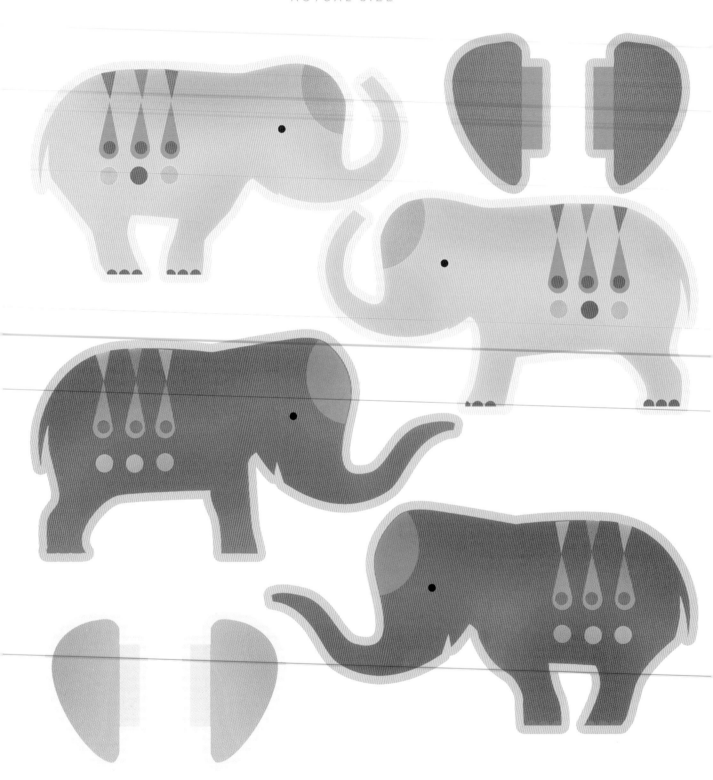

ABOUT THE DESIGNERS

Alli Bartkowski teaches and writes on the forefront of the quilling industry with her creative kits and innovative tools. Her company, Quilled Creations, Inc. (quilledcreations.com), is the world's leading supplier of paper quilling products. Alli is a member of the Craft & Hobby Association and is an accredited member of the North American Quilling Guild. Alli is the author of *Paper Quilling for the First Time, Nifty 50 Quilled Cards,* and *Quilled Flowers.*

Amanda Carestio is one busy lady. She's a writer, sewist, quilter, crocheter, mama, editor, and dog lover (especially brindles!), based in the beautiful mountains of Asheville, North Carolina. Amanda has been creating since she can remember. She's new to paper cutting, but she's fallen in love hard and is excited to have another crafting supply to hoard. Amanda is the author of several Lark/Sterling books including *Never Been Stitched, Fa La La La Felt, Felt-o-ween,* and many more.

Candie Cooper is a designer with a passion for bold colors and twisting and turning materials until they sing. "I'm inspired by so many things. Most of all, I want my work to tell a story. A place I want to visit, a nostalgic memory from childhood, romance and more . . . it's all in my creations." She is the author of *Earringology, Necklaceology, Metalworking 101 for Beaders,* and *Felted Jewelry.* She's appeared on Jewelry Television's "Jewel School" and the PBS series "Beads, Baubles, and Jewels." Visit her website and blog at candiecooper.com for craft tutorials and a peek into her everyday life.

Ellen Deakin is the cofounder of Happythought, an online store and blog full of craft ideas and fun printable paper crafts. She met Harry Olden at the Glasgow School of Art and, after a decade of working in the design and music industry, they launched Happythought. They are currently based in Chile with their two young children, Harvey and Missy, who are a constant source of inspiration and the perfect guinea pigs (and sometime models) for new creations and craft tutorials. At Happythought, the emphasis is on producing paper craft templates that, as well as being lovely to look at, are easy to make, with the minimum of fuss and the maximum of fun. You can find more fun paper craft projects, party printables, and craft tutorials at happythought.co.uk.

Silvina De Vita is an Argentinean multi-skilled artist based in London. With a range of experience in graphic design, digital art, painting, illustration, and paper sculpture, she combines her artistic talents and inspirations to create exciting and engaging art. Her project of the moment is the production of 3D sculptures, made using textured paper and wire and presented in hand-made white wooden boxes and glass domes. These elaborate designs show not only Silvina's technical skill, but also her artistic vision—look closely enough into these small boxes and you are drawn into the worlds of the silhouetted characters contained within. See more of her work at SilvinaDeVita.com.

Ali Harrison is the owner of the Light and Paper Shop in Toronto, Ontario. Ali has always loved creating art, but didn't discover her passion for paper cutting until 2012. Ali loves being able to create paper cutting art in large and small form, everything from large-scale pieces that span an entire wall to simple cards to give a friend. Ali is excited that in addition to sharing her work, she can inspire others to try their hand at their own paper creations. See more of her creations at LightandPaperShop.com and on Etsy.

Dee Dee Jacq has a Bachelor of Fine Arts degree, and she's always had the desire to create and express her own visions and dreams of the natural world, the place where she can escape from the day-to-day grind, recharge her batteries, meditate, and forget the problems of the day. Dee Dee is currently exploring our natural world through various mediums such as photography, pastels, mixed media, printmaking, clay, and new to the mix paper sculpture. Her paper sculpture, pastels, and photography purely serve a surreal aesthetic. She hopes that her art inspires your own dreams and visions.

Rebecca Kedborn is an artist, journalist, photographer, and Etsy shop owner living on the Swedish west coast near Gothenburg, Sweden's second largest town. Living in the countryside, Rebecca finds nature to be large source of inspiration. She also has a great fascination for architecture and buildings. With paper as her favorite craft material, she designs paper lanterns inspired by American and European cities. Rebecca is also the owner of the popular blog Rebecca's DIY (www.rebeccasdiy.se).

Carlos N. Molina is a Puerto Rican artist, designer, and author living and working in New York City. Since childhood, Carlos's favorite medium has been paper, and today his work is known for its irresistible charm and imaginative engineering. His paper art has been exhibited in Puerto Rico, New York, Chicago, Los Angeles, Portugal, Belgium, South Korea, Japan, Hong Kong, and Shanghai. It has been included in El Museo del Barrio Biennal, The Paper Art International Catalogue, and the annual *Art and Faith of the Crèche Show*. He has been featured on HGTV and in numerous art and design blogs. More examples of his innovative paper cutting designs can be seen online at CarlosNMolina. com and in his popular book *Creating Kirigami*, also published by Sterling Publishing.

Stephanie Paxman is a creative blogger from Washington state. From a young age, she's tried everything, including needle crafts, drawing, sewing, watercolor, decoupage, painting, and, of course, paper crafts. She loves bright colors, metallic, and glitter, and believes that everyone can throw a personal twist on any craft. You can find more of her work at CraftingintheRain.com.

Cynthia Shaffer is a mixed media artist, creative sewist, and photographer whose love of art can be traced back to childhood. After earning a degree in textiles from California State University, Long Beach, Cynthia worked for 10 years as the owner of a company that specialized in the design and manufacture of sportswear. Numerous books and magazines have featured Cynthia's art and photography work: she is the author of *Stash Happy Patchwork* (Lark, 2011), *Stash Happy Appliqué* (Lark, 2012), and co-author of *Serge It!* (Lark 2014). In her spare time, Cynthia knits, crochets, paints, and dabbles in all sorts of crafts. If she's not crafting, Cynthia can been found at the gym lifting weights or kick boxing. Cynthia lives with her husband Scott, sons Corry and Cameron, and beloved dogs Harper and Berklee in Southern California. For more information, visit Cynthia online at CynthiaShaffer.typepad. com or CynthiaShaffer.com.

Regina Squier's family didn't have much money when she was growing up, so she and her sister would look around the house for items that they could up-cycle and turn into toys. They would take a toilet paper roll and make a doll, or turn a cereal box into doll furniture. It wasn't long before they started coming up with crafty ideas to sell door to door to make a little bit of money to buy more craft supplies. Through the years, Regina learned crochet, quilling, photography, cross stitch, and sewing, but her current hobby is paper crafting. She makes and sells a large variety of paper flowers on Etsy. Find more of her work at PapersAndPetals.Etsy.com.

INDEX